Three Wheelers

Malcolm Bobbitt

VELOCE PUBLISHING
THE PUBLISHER OF FINE AUTOMOTIVE BOOKS

Also from Veloce Publishing:
SpeedPro Series
4-Cylinder Engine - How to Blueprint & Build a Short Block for High Performance by Des Hammill
Alfa Romeo Twin Cam Engines - How to Power Tune by Jim Kartalamakis
BMC 998cc A-Series Engine - How to Power Tune by Des Hammill
BMC/Rover 1275cc A-Series Engines - How to Power Tune by Des Hammill
Camshafts - How to Choose & Time them for Maximum Power by Des Hammill
Cylinder Heads - How to Build, Modify & Power Tune Second Edition by Peter Burgess
Distributor-type Ignition Systems - How to Build & Power Tune by Des Hammill
Fast Road Car - How to Plan and Build by Daniel Stapleton
Ford SOHC 'Pinto' & Sierra Cosworth DOHC Engines - How to Power Tune Updated & Revised Edition
by Des Hammill
Ford V8 - How to Power Tune Small Block Engines by Des Hammill
Harley-Davidson Evolution Engines - How to Build & Power Tune by Des Hammill
Holley Carburetors - How to Build & Power Tune by Des Hammill
Jaguar XK Engines - How to Power Tune by Des Hammill
MG Midget & Austin-Healey Sprite - How to Power Tune Updated Edition by Daniel Stapleton
MGB 4-Cylinder Engine - How to Power Tune by Peter Burgess
MGB - How to Give your MGB V8 Power Updated & Revised Edition by Roger Williams
MGB, MGC & MGB V8 - How to Improve by Roger Williams
Mini Engines - How to Power Tune on a Small Budget by Des Hammill
Motorsport - Getting Started in by Sam Collins
Rover V8 Engines - How to Power Tune by Des Hammill
Sportscar/Kitcar Suspension & Brakes - How to Build & Modify by Des Hammill
SU Carburettors - How to Build & Modify for High Performance by Des Hammill
Tiger Avon Sportscar - How to Build Your Own by Jim Dudley
TR2, 3 & TR4 - How to Improve by Roger Williams
TR5, 250 & TR6 - How to Improve by Roger Williams
V8 Engine - How to Build a Short Block for High Performance by Des Hammill
Volkswagen Beetle Suspension, Brakes & Chassis - How to Modify for High Performance by James Hale
Volkswagen Bus Suspension, Brakes & Chassis - How to Modify for High Performance by James Hale
Weber DCOE, & Dellorto DHLA Carburetors - How to Build & Power Tune Third Edition by Des Hammill

Colour Family Album Series
Alfa Romeo by Andrea & David Sparrow
Bubblecars & Microcars by Andrea & David Sparrow
Bubblecars & Microcars, More by Andrea & David Sparrow
Citroen 2CV by Andrea & David Sparrow
Citroen DS by Andrea & David Sparrow
Custom VWs by Andrea & David Sparrow
Fiat & Abarth 500 & 600 by Andrea & David Sparrow
Lambretta by Andrea & David Sparrow
Mini & Mini Cooper by Andrea & David Sparrow
Motor Scooters by Andrea & David Sparrow
Porsche by Andrea & David Sparrow
Triumph Sportscars by Andrea & David Sparrow
Vespa by Andrea & David Sparrow
VW Beetle by Andrea & David Sparrow
VW Bus, Camper, Van & Pick-up by Andrea & David Sparrow
VW Custom Beetle by Andrea & David Sparrow

General
AC Two-litre Saloons & Buckand Sportscars by Leo Archibald
Alfa Romeo Berlinas (Saloons/Sedans) by John Tipler
Alfa Romeo Giulia Coupe GT & GTA by John Tipler
Anatomy of the Works Minis by Brian Moylan
Automotive A-Z, Lane's Dictionary of Automotive Terms by Keith Lane
Automotive Mascots by David Kay & Lynda Springate
Bentley Continental, Corniche and Azure, by Martin Bennett
BMW 5-Series by Marc Cranswick
BMW Z-Cars by James Taylor
British Cars, The Complete Catalogue of, 1895-1975 by Culshaw & Horrobin
British Police Cars by Nick Walker
Caravans, The Illustrated History 1919-1959 by Andrew Jenkinson
Caravans, The Illustrated History from 1960 by Andrew Jenkinson
Bugatti Type 40 by Barrie Price
Bugatti 46/50 Updated Edition by Barrie Price
Bugatti 57 2nd Edition - by Barrie Price

Caravanning & Trailer Tenting, the Essential Handbook by Len Archer
Chrysler 300 - America's Most Powerful Car by Robert Ackerson
Cobra - The Real Thing! by Trevor Legate
Cortina - Ford's Bestseller by Graham Robson
Coventry Climax Racing Engines by Des Hammill
Daimler SP250 'Dart' by Brian Long
Datsun/Nissan 280ZX & 300ZX by Brian Long
Datsun Z - From Fairlady to 280Z by Brian Long
Dune Buggy Phenomenon by James Hale
Dune Buggies by James Hale
Fiat & Abarth 124 Spider & Coupe by John Tipler
Fiat & Abarth 500 & 600 Second edition by Malcolm Bobbitt
Ford F100/F150 Pick-up by Robert Ackerson
Ford GT40 by Trevor Legate
Ford Model Y by Sam Roberts
Harley-Davidson, Growing up by Jean Davidson
Jaguar XJ-S, by Brian Long
Karmann-Ghia Coupe & Convertible by Malcolm Bobbitt
Land Rover, The Half-Ton Military by Mark Cook
Lea-Francis Story, The by Barrie Price
Lexus Story, The by Brian Long
Lola - The Illustrated History (1957-1977) by John Starkey
Lola - All The Sports Racing & Single-Seater Racing Cars 1978-1997 by John Starkey
Lola T70 - The Racing History & Individual Chassis Record 3rd Edition by John Starkey
Lotus 49 by Michael Oliver
Mazda MX-5/Miata 1.6 Enthusiast's Workshop Manual by Rod Grainger & Pete Shoemark
Mazda MX-5/Miata 1.8 Enthusiast's Workshop Manual by Rod Grainger & Pete Shoemark
Mazda MX-5 (& Eunos Roadster) - The World's Favourite Sportscar by Brian Long
MGA by John Price Williams
MGB & MGB GT - Expert Guide (Auto-Doc Series) by Roger Williams
Mini Cooper - The Real Thing! by John Tipler
Mitsubishi Lancer Evo by Brian Long
Motor Racing at Goodwood in the Sixties by Tony Gardiner
Motorhomes, The Illustrated History by Andrew Jenkinson
MR2 - Toyota's Mid-engined Sports Car by Brian Long
Pontiac Firebird by Marc Cranswick
Porsche 356 by Brian Long
Porsche 911R, RS & RSR, 4th Ed. by John Starkey
Porsche 911 - The Definitive History 1963-1971 by Brian Long
Porsche 911 - The Definitive History 1971-1977 by Brian Long
Porsche 911 - The Definitive History 1977-1987 by Brian Long
Porsche 911 - The Definitive History 1987-1997 by Brian Long
Porsche 914 & 914-6 by Brian Long
Porsche 924 by Brian Long
Porsche 944 by Brian Long
Rolls-Royce Silver Shadow/Bentley T Series Corniche & Camargue Updated Edition by Malcolm Bobbitt
Rolls-Royce Silver Spirit, Silver Spur & Bentley Mulsanne by Malcolm Bobbitt
Rolls-Royce Silver Wraith, Dawn & Cloud/Bentley MkVI, R & S Series
by Martyn Nutland
RX-7 - Mazda's Rotary Engine Sportscar by Brian Long
Singer Story: Cars, Commercial Vehicles, Bicycles & Motorcycles by Kevin Atkinson
Subaru Impreza by Brian Long
Taxi! The Story of the 'London' Taxicab by Malcolm Bobbitt
Three Wheelers by Malcolm Bobbitt
Triumph Motorcycles & the Meriden Factory by Hughie Hancox
Triumph Tiger Cub Bible by Mike Estall
Triumph Trophy Bible by Harry Woolridge
Triumph TR2/3/3A, How to Restore, by Roger Williams
Triumph TR4/4A, How to Restore, by Roger Williams
Triumph TR5/250 & 6, How to Restore, by Roger Williams
Triumph TR6 by William Kimberley
Turner's Triumphs, Edward Turner & his Triumph Motorcycles by Jeff Clew
Velocette Motorcycles - MSS to Thruxton by Rod Burris
Volkswagens of the World by Simon Glen
VW Beetle Cabriolet by Malcolm Bobbitt
VW Beetle - The Car of the 20th Century by Richard Copping
VW Bus, Camper, Van, Pickup by Malcolm Bobbitt
Works Rally Mechanic by Brian Moylan

First published in 2003 by Veloce Publishing Limited, 33 Trinity Street, Dorchester DT1 1TT, England.
Fax 01305 268864/e-mail info@veloce.co.uk/web www.veloce.co.uk or www.velocebooks.com
ISBN 1-903706-81-5/UPC 36847-00281-7

Readers with ideas for automotive books, or books on other transport or related hobby subjects, are invited to write to the editorial director of Veloce Publishing at the above address.
British Library Cataloguing in Publication Data - A catalogue record for this book is available from the British Library.

Typesetting (URW Imperial T), design and page make-up all by Veloce Publishing Ltd on Apple Mac. Printed in Croatia.

Contents

The Hon. Leopold Canning pictured aboard his 5hp Century tandem (which is fully equipped for touring) at Ballater in the autumn of 1901 whilst driving from Aberdeen to London. The Century had been introduced in 1899 by Ralph Jackson, a cycle maker from Altrincham in Cheshire, and in 1901 the firm moved to Willesden in north London. As well as Century vehicles, the company produced tricars under the Eagle name. (Author's collection, source unknown)

3

Three Wheelers

In competitive events the Léon Bollée enjoyed some success and was held in high regard by none other than The Hon. C.S. Rolls of Rolls-Royce fame. The car's achievements were largely responsible for the Metropolitan Police acquiring an example to conduct trials in the late 1890s to establish whether it might prove beneficial in policing London's streets. The Margate Constabulary was another police force which evaluated the machine. In this artist's impression the vehicle's controls are clearly evident, the lever on the driver's left being the brake and gear selector. A small wheel on the right steered the car. (Metropolitan Police)

Introduction

Three wheelers, often perceived as being somewhat peculiar, have contributed enormously to motoring history. Rather than being consigned to a past era and serving as alternatives to 'proper cars', they have, with the benefit of developing technology, a future as fuel-efficient means of transport.

Mention three wheelers and the image of Morgans, Bond Minicars and Reliants comes to mind. Bubblecars, too, are recalled, with Isettas, Heinkels and Messerschmitts among others. Vespas and Piaggios are the staple diets of many Western European commercial markets while a wealth of new ideas are emerging from Volkswagen and other giant car producers.

Three wheelers mean different things to different people. How many motorists had three wheelers as their

Is it surprising that the sight of Edward Pennington aboard his Torpedo with two passengers and the driver perched at the rear was the cause of much interest? Pennington was regarded as a confidence trickster while his motor tricycle was considered as being somewhat lethal in operation. The fact that it worked at all is something of a wonder! (Author's collection, source unknown)

The earliest petrol-driven three wheeler is the Petro-Cycle which Edward Butler patented in 1884. The design was shown the following year at an inventions exhibition but it was not until 1887 that a working example was built with a four-stroke engine replacing the two-stroke two-cylinder version. The transmission, too, was developed from direct drive which meant that when the vehicle was doing 12mph the engine was turning at only 100rpm. By interposing a reduction gear it was possible to achieve a ratio of 6:1. Like many inventions Butler's Petro-Cycle was destined to obscurity when the machine was scrapped due to the lack of enthusiasm for his invention. (Author's collection)

first car? And what about those who progressed from motorcycles to sidecar outfits and ultimately to the three wheelers which offered so much practicality without compromising financial investment or fuel economy?

In the dawn of motoring three wheelers afforded a means of independence much greater than bicycles or motorcycles, and when it came to long-distance travel what was better than a Morgan with its sporting pedigree? BSAs, Coventry Victors and Raleigh Safety Sevens offered families economical transport, and for those drivers more involved with the sporting scene these little cars were capable performers.

After World War Two few were able to obtain or

afford new cars, and even then these were subject to severe fuel rationing. With raw material shortages and manufacturing limitations three wheelers came into their own when innovative engineers produced designs utilising substitute resources. Their offerings were inexpensive to build and economical to run.

Some of those products may appear impractical now but at the time they were wholly viable. With relatively few pre-war vehicles on the road Bond and Reliant three wheelers afforded welcome transport. The fact that these vehicles relied on simple technology did not matter, and being uncomplicated made them all the more appealing for they could be easily maintained with little expense.

Despite three wheelers' apparent lack of

The Singer Tri-Voiturette was introduced in 1901 as a tri-car with front-wheel drive. The photograph shows Edwin Perks, the vehicle's designer, during trials conducted for The Autocar. Sitting in the basket is Perk's wife and young daughter. The Tri-Voiturette could be adapted as a commercial carrier with a trunk fitted in place of the passenger seat. (Author's collection)

sophistication, owners were not deterred from embarking on ambitious treks to the furthermost points of the British Isles. Contemporary motoring journals reveal remarkable expeditions throughout mainland Europe and beyond, and what is evident is that three wheelers were notably reliable.

Whilst the sight of three wheelers being nonchalantly driven along Britain's highways undoubtedly produces comment, complimentary or otherwise, it is pertinent to realise how many of these workhorses were bought by enthusiasts. Some 300,000 were built in Britain, and in excess of a quarter of million were produced abroad.

That is not the end of the story. Three wheelers provide essential and economical transport for many thousands of people and traders in Asia and the Indian sub-continent, while nearer to home a proliferation of retro three wheelers capturing the style of 1920s and '30s motoring are becoming popular.

Acknowledgements

I am grateful to the following individuals, enthusiasts and organisations who have assisted in the preparation of this book. Andrew Minney; Gordon Fitzgerald; Jonathan Day (photographic librarian, National Motor Museum); BMW; Volkswagen (UK); Douglas Ferreira; Graham Hull; Ivana Birkettova; Metropolitan Police; David Herrod and those owners who allowed me to photograph their vehicles. Not least, my thanks to my wife Jean for her usual patience regarding motoring matters, and to Rod Grainger who suggested I compile this work. A number of images are from my own collection that I have amassed over a number of years. The original source of some are unknown.

Malcolm Bobbitt
Cumbria

Three Wheelers Before 1939

The development of the bicycle and tricycle, together with the quest for motorised transport, led Edward Butler to demonstrate his Petro-Cycle in the mid-1880s. Butler's design, though arguably a motorcycle, was highly sophisticated for its time and original drawings depict a single rear wheel driven by a horizontal two-cylinder two-stroke engine. In 1887 Butler decided to improve the performance of his machine by replacing the engine with a four-stroke affair and that the direct drive transmission be superseded by an epicyclic reduction gear.

Edward Butler's invention did not go into production after its appearance at the 1887 Stanley Cycle Show. He destroyed the vehicle on becoming demoralised by Britain's reluctance to acknowledge the arrival of the motorcar which had become firmly established elsewhere in Europe. The motorised tricycle did eventually enjoy some popularity and the De Dion-Bouton of 1898 was one that was highly regarded. More than 15,000 De Dion-Boutons were manufactured in

Forecars enjoyed some popularity during the early Twentieth Century. As well as being built by some of the better known manufacturers they were constructed by cycle makers intent on diversifying into more sophisticated machinery. This vehicle was the product of William Ireland of Sankey in Cheshire, a well known and highly respected bicycle manufacturer trading under the Walton name. The Walton forecar exhibited at Manchester received good reviews. (Murial Cuppage)

Racing tricycles achieved some popularity in the early 1900s and in November 1901 Monsieur Osmont endeavoured to take the mile in under a minute with his De Dion-Bouton at the Parc Agricole d'Archères near Paris. After several attempts Osmont succeeded with a time of 58.35 seconds. (Author's collection)

France over a period of six years where tricycle racing emerged as a popular sport.

Edward Butler was neither the first nor the sole inventor and engineer to propose three-wheeled transport. Nicholas Cugnot's steam-driven leviathan of 1769 was hardly a realistic contender in the personal

Taking the place of the horse, the Ivel agricultural motor is being used for ploughing. Powered by a 10hp engine, this early tractor was designed for heavy use and rough work and presumably the well-attired operatives were dressed appropriately in the interest of publicity. The Ivel could function as a road tractor and as a stationary engine and was easier to handle than a steam engine.
(Author's collection)

travel stakes, but Karl Benz's Patent-Motorwagen of 1888 showed the way forward. The three-wheeled motorcar was born!

Before the turn of the century several designs of three wheelers came into prominence, some of which were relatively short lived while others emerged to feature as leading names in the motor industry. Among those to quickly fall into obscurity was the Pennington Torpedo of 1896, as this was a dubious machine with an unconvincing record for reliability.

An American, Edward Joel Pennington made all sorts of claims regarding motor vehicle inventions, few of which ever materialised. The Torpedo was one that did and has since been described as one of the least successful designs to have functioned on British roads. Pennington's designs lacked sophistication and the fact that his machines performed at all was miraculous. It is all the more incredible that he convinced others his inventions were technically superior to anything else, and managed to extract £100,000 from financier and engineer Harry Lawson, who was behind a scheme to monopolise Britain's fledgling motor industry.

Harry Lawson was synonymous with Coventry, the home of the British cycle and motorcar industries. His name was linked with The Great Horseless Carriage Co. Ltd., Daimler, Humber and Léon Bollée. The Léon Bollée enjoyed some distinction for, whilst it was primitive, it performed well enough and commanded greater speeds than any other vehicle of its time.

In November 1896 two Bollées participated in the first London to Brighton run and took first and second places. The leading car took 3 hours, 44 minutes and 35 seconds to complete the journey from London's Metropole Hotel to Brighton's seafront. In terms of motor sport the Léon Bollée had few rivals and attracted such prominent motorists as The Hon. Charles Rolls, later of Rolls-Royce fame. In 1897 he drove a Bollée from London to Cambridge, which was all the more challenging as the run was made at night. Whilst

Pictured at work in London's streets in 1903 this *Eagle Carrier* is in service with the Post Office to convey mail between the North-West and South-West postal districts. Journeys were made hourly between the two post offices, which meant that the vehicle was kept hard at work throughout each day. The Eagle, which was manufactured by the Eagle Engineering and Motor Co., predates the Auto-Carrier which was of a similar design. Tests conducted by the Post Office and Eagle Engineering showed the vehicle with its 4½hp De Dion engine and two-speed transmission to be capable of carrying 6cwt of wet sand, which is nearly double the weight of mail that was usually transported. (Author's collection)

Rolls was at first enthusiastic towards the Bollée he nevertheless grew to be critical towards its crude design and appetite for the soldering iron!

The Léon Bollée also received attention from Britain's police forces. Both Margate Constabulary and the Metropolitan anticipated that such machines would speed beat duties and improve communications. Handling the Bollée called for some particular skills for it proved to be precarious in wet weather and on greasy surfaces. Steering was via a small hand wheel on the driver's right, and braking - which at times could be very uncertain - was controlled by a lever positioned on the opposite side of the car. To make things difficult the brake lever not only operated the clutch but also selected gear speeds. Racing driver Sammy Davis, who will always be associated with driving Bentleys at Le Mans, owned an example in the late 1920s and often took it to race meetings as a means of entertainment.

The first Wolseley car designed by Herbert Austin owed its origins to the Bollée. Austin visited France to study the French motor industry and believed most of the machines he saw were too heavy and clumsy, except the Bollée brothers' motor tricycle. Instead of adopting the single-cylinder engine of the French vehicle he opted for a 2hp twin-cylinder air-cooled unit, and in place of a steering wheel he chose a tiller. Austin also adopted modified braking and transmission systems in addition to independent rear suspension. The second Wolseley was very different with the single wheel at the front in the style of a bath chair. Steered via a tiller it provided seating for two with the driver and passenger sitting back-to-back.

The Léon Bollée design was also taken up by Humber which built the cars under licence. Harry Lawson paid £20,000 for the English manufacturing and patent rights. A variant on the original design was the Humber

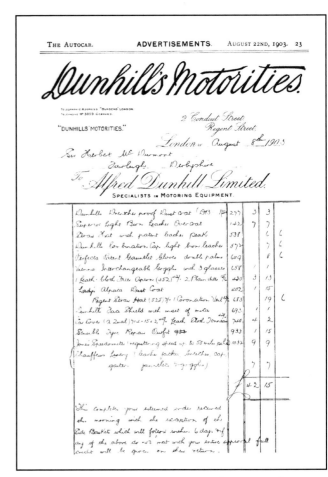

In the early days of motoring drivers of all types of motor vehicle were subjected to the vagaries of the elements. Companies such as Alfred Dunhill specialised in supplying all types of motoring equipment, including clothing as this advertisement from August 1903 depicts. Vienna Interchangeable Goggles with three glasses cost one guinea. (Author's collection)

For Work
or Play on
the Great
Highway.

Morgan Runabout

Stand No. 53

Prices from
£95 to £147

Send for List and name of nearest agent
MORGAN MOTOR CO., LTD
MALVERN LINK

*Morgans are often accepted as being the archetypal vintage
three wheeler, and for very good reason as they acquired
a special place in motoring history. What makes Morgan
so special is its design which, whilst conceived to afford
economical motoring, nevertheless lent itself to being an able
competitor in motor sport trials and events. This charming
period advertisement really does sum-up the Morgan ethos.
(Author's collection)*

Motor Sociable which was introduced in 1899, so-called because it allowed the driver and passenger to sit side-by-side.

In the opening years of the Twentieth Century Riley produced tricars which were developed from its 1899 motor tricycle. These looked more like motorcycles but with two wheels forward supporting a passenger seat and the driver sitting aft upon a saddle steering via handlebars. With development the Riley became more sophisticated. Handlebars gave way to a wheel while engine sizes progressed from 3hp to 6hp.

Lagonda was another well-known manufacturer to build tricars. Wilbur Gunn, an American whose main interests were engineering and opera, established his motorcycle business at Staines in Middlesex and in 1904 began building three wheelers before deciding to concentrate on building four-wheeled cars.

There was also a profusion of cycle manufacturers entering the tricar market. Many produced only a handful of machines before going out of business. One of the more successful was William Ireland, the builder of the Walton bicycle at Sankey in Cheshire. Ireland's machines were exhibited at the Manchester Motor Show in 1902 and were admired for their quality.

One of the most famous cycle makers to diversify into tricar manufacturing was Singer with its Tri-voiturette. Employing front-wheel drive, courtesy of the Motor Wheel, the driver and passenger sat in tandem back to back; by adopting rear wheel drive the passenger sat at the front in an upholstered wicker basket, and the machine was termed a forecar. Soon after Singer started building motorcars in 1904 it announced its 6hp machine, and later the more powerful 9hp which, by the standards of the time was highly sophisticated with a three-speed transmission.

1904 was the year when the wooden-framed Auto-

Three Wheelers

Left: This Sporting Runabout fitted with a JAP 964cc 8hp engine is one of the earliest surviving Morgan three wheelers. Although the first Morgan cars were shown in 1910 it was not until 1912 that the Morgan Motor Company was formed. The same year this example was built. (Author's collection)

Right: There exists a huge amount of enthusiasm for Morgan three wheelers with owners intent on using their cars for the purpose they were designed. Several engine types were specified over the years, the JAP being the most popular. Others were supplied by MAG, Anzani, Blackburne, Green, and Precision. (Author's collection)

The thoroughness of the Morgan's fundamental design was responsible for its popularity and therefore long production run. In addition to being built at Malvern, Morgans were also constructed in France by Darmont et Badelogue at Courbevoie, Morgan having granted a licence to the French firm in 1919. Darmont had no difficulty selling the cars and produced several hundred a year throughout the Twenties. High performance models fitted with supercharged Blackburne engines could attain speeds of 100mph. This alluring piece of publicity material first appeared in 1923 courtesy of Léo Bouillon and effectively illustrates the charm of three wheeling. Another French version of the Morgan three-wheeler was the Sandford, which was built in Paris at Levallois. Although it never sold in the same numbers as its Courbevoie rival, the Sandford was, however, a capable performer in motor sport events and was acclaimed for its build quality (Author's collection)

Reliability and economy contributed to Morgan's formidable reputation. Along with this the car attracted those with a carefree disposition which is portrayed in this delightful piece of publicity material gracing the cover of *The Book of the Morgan*. In today's money 2/6d represents 12½p, which gives a clue as to the vintage of the item. (Author's collection)

Carrier went into production. The Auto-Carrier, a three-wheeled delivery truck with its storage compartment supported by the front wheels and a 636cc air-cooled single-cylinder engine beneath the driver's seat, sold in substantial numbers. They were bought by some of the leading retailers of the day including Army & Navy Stores, Boots the Chemist, Dickens & Jones, and Selfridges. A passenger version, the AC Sociable, appeared in 1907, and examples were seen competing in a number of reliability events around the country including Brooklands.

The one three wheeler, appearing before 1914, to have great impact on the motoring society was the Morgan. The prototype Morgan Runabout was built in 1909 and made its debut at the 1910 Motor Cycle Show at Olympia where it was greeted with lukewarm enthusiasm. What prospective customers wanted was a reliable machine to accommodate two people. H.F.S. Morgan soon saw to it that his Runabout made its mark at various reliability trials, and within a year

Right: The wide track of this JAP-engined Morgan indicates that the vehicle has been used for racing. Some cars were built with a wider track to customer specification but a number have been rebuilt for such purpose. What is not entirely evident in this photograph is the Super Sports body styling. (Author's collection)

In 1935 Morgan introduced the F-Type three-wheeler which had a 933cc Ford Model Y side valve engine. Other features of the car included more accommodating two or four-seater bodywork and a pressed steel chassis to replace the previous tubular type. The Ford engine was concealed beneath the bonnet and afforded somewhat smoother performance than did the air-cooled V-twin models. The F-Type also formed the basis of the four-wheeled Morgan, which was developed largely in response to a threat by the government of the day to abolish the horse-power tax from which three wheelers benefited.
(Author's collection)

Three Wheelers

BSAs were highly regarded for their performance and reliability and, like Morgan, adopted the single rear wheel principle. Unlike their Malvern rival, BSA adopted front wheel drive for its three wheelers. BSA introduced its three wheeler in 1929 with a one-litre air-cooled V-twin engine that was based on a Hotchkiss design dating to 1921. When London traffic patrols were introduced in the early 1930s the Metropolitan Police acquired some of these vehicles, an example of which is seen here leaving Scotland Yard. (Metropolitan Police)

and provided reliable and inexpensive motoring, and their rise in popularity heralded the formation of the Cyclecar Club in 1912. Throughout Britain and Europe three wheelers provided vital transport for both domestic and commercial purposes.

During the inter-war years Morgans were the principal three wheelers which, as well as providing an economic means of transport, were highly successful in motor sport. To say that Morgans had few rivals would be incorrect as there emerged a proliferation of three-wheeled cyclecars, some of which enjoyed more success than others. Of the more eccentric there was the tiny Chertsey-built Xtra which was little more than a motorised sidecar, while the seemingly impractical Harper Runabout was more akin to a scooter. The

With two burly policemen aboard, the BSA offered little in the way of comfort or spaciousness. Although their performance was sufficiently proven in sporting events, such cars patrolling London's congested streets offered an amusing spectacle. (Metropolitan Police)

had introduced a two-seater model which was widely acclaimed and he was overwhelmed with orders.

The cyclecar movement became firmly established just before World War One. A plethora of simple and often crude designs emerged from an excess of manufacturers, many of which went out of business as quickly as they had arrived. A good number of cyclecars were three wheelers, which were hybrids that went a stage farther than motorcycle combinations but stopped short of being proper motorcars. Some were well made

Established in the 1870s, Raleigh was highly respected
for its bicycles and motorcycles and in the early 1930s
ventured into car production with the Raleigh Safety Seven.
The vehicle was in production for only a short time, Raleigh
deciding to concentrate on two-wheeled transport. Tom
Williams, the Safety Seven's designer, parted company with
Raleigh to set up business building Reliant three wheelers.
(National Motor Museum)

fragile-looking Cambro took on the appearance of a
child's pedal car, but few machines could challenge
Jürgen Skafte Rasmussen's DKW rickshaw-type van with
its 594cc twin-cylinder two-stroke engine driving the
single front wheel.

There, were, however, more sophisticated offerings,
many of which acquired a reputation. The Coventry
Victor, unkindly referred to as the 'Country Vicar', proved
popular, as did Raleigh's Safety Seven which provided
adequate and economical motoring for smaller families.
The CWS Bell and D'yrsan were both good performers
but it was the BSA that was particularly sought after and
which did well in competitive events. A number of BSAs
were purchased by the Metropolitan Police to serve as
traffic patrol vehicles. A role they fulfilled competently
despite their diminutive size.

It was the short-lived Raleigh Safety Seven that set
the scene for the future development. When production
was discontinued, in order for Raleigh to concentrate on
cycle and motorcycle manufacturing, Tom Williams, the
car's designer, left Raleigh to establish the Reliant Motor
Company at Tamworth where he built three-wheeler
vans based on the Safety Seven's design.

Post-war Austerity

The urgency to resume motor vehicle production after the War was severely compromised for not only were there shortages of raw materials but also the motor industry was denied sustained and secure investment. The need to export a high proportion of all the vehicles that Britain produced in the interest of earning foreign currency was explained, on behalf of the government, in 1945 by Sir Stafford Cripps, then President of the Board of Trade. He foresaw that manufacturers should concentrate on mass-producing a relatively few key designs that would be internationally sought after rather than build wide ranges of models in moderate numbers. Behind the scenes at Whitehall, there were even proposals to nationalise Britain's motor industry.

When Tom Williams established Reliant Engineering at Tamworth before World War Two he began producing three-wheeled vans that owed as much to motorcycle technology as they did motorcars. They appealed to traders who wanted a basic and inexpensive form of transport, and, more importantly. holders of motorcycle licences could drive them. Few early Reliants survive, this being seen at a vintage vehicle rally. (Gordon Fitzgerald)

One of the first three wheelers to emerge after World War Two was the French-built Mathis. Emile Mathis unveiled his first car in 1910 and during the inter-war years produced a wide range of luxury cars and commercial vehicles. Anticipating the need for economy cars he devised this small aerodynamic machine capable of 94mpg. The 333 (3 wheels, 3 seats, 3 litres per 100km) was displayed at the 1946 Paris Salon and although a number of prototypes were built, the car never went into production. (National Motor Museum)

Motor manufacturers nevertheless went their own way, and for a decade Britain was the largest exporter of motor vehicles. Despite the industry earning substantial foreign revenue, the massive export drive, with output geared to steel allocation, deprived the home market of cars that were more easily affordable and available. Although the Morris Minor was produced in large numbers, opportunities were missed in the rush to export. This left few resources for car makers to design new models. It was mainly pre-war designs that were delivered around the world to car-hungry motorists, while foreign manufacturers, such as Volkswagen, Fiat

The first Reliant vans used JAP V-twin engines but ultimately Tom Williams decided to utilise the Austin Seven unit, which is seen here. The chassis layout is simple, and being underslung at the rear allowed for a low loading arrangement. When Austin discontinued production of its 747cc side valve engine Tom Williams designed a similar engine which was built by Reliant at Tamworth. (National Motor Museum)

Reliant Regent vans were built in a number of styles to suit customer requirement, including this Veg-e-Car mobile shop. The layout of the vehicle called for some ingenuity from its designer. (National Motor Museum)

and Renault captured home sales.

Although the first post-war motor show held in the autumn of 1948 attracted more than half a million visitors, for most of them owning a car was little short of a pipe-dream. There was up to three-year waiting lists for deliveries of home market cars, and then orders were subject to purchase tax which increased prices by a third, and two-thirds for those cars in excess of 1000cc. When a car was eventually delivered there was the matter of petrol rationing ...

In times of austerity, the dearth of truly inexpensive personal transport gave rise to all sorts of ideas and inventions, some more sophisticated than others. It is not surprising that some pretty radical designs emerged as economy was the main consideration in respect of materials, construction and running costs.

Despite some novel ideas, mainly from France and Germany, to cater for a demand that not even the Volkswagen Beetle and Citroën 2CV could satisfy, it was the British that so successfully endorsed the three wheeler market to offer practical alternatives to conventional four-wheelers.

Two names that emerged, synonymous with budget motoring, were Bond and Reliant. Both firms grew to enjoy substantial sales and acquired respectability. The immediate post-war era sustained several manufacturers in the economy car market, but in the more prosperous sixties and seventies the demand for what was perceived as peculiar little three wheelers began to diminish.

Bond and Reliant were by no means the only contenders in the minicar stakes. There were a number of manufacturers, some of which were highly regarded for their sports cars, that decided it was necessary to diversify production if they were to remain in business. Prominent names such as Allard and AC, therefore, became associated with three wheeler motoring, but

Post-war austerity provoked Lawrie Bond to design his Minicar in 1948. It was very small and powered by nothing more powerful than a Villiers 122cc motorcycle engine and gearbox mounted in unit with the single front wheel. There was no necessity for doors but protection from the elements was afforded by a rudimentary hood. The Bond on the right is a Mark D with the more powerful Villiers 197cc single-cylinder two-stroke engine. (National Motor Museum)

not entirely with the success they anticipated. There were also some brave attempts at marketing three wheelers that were directly aimed at providing the most minimal motoring, and none more so than by football pools promoter Vernons. Its odd little Gordon with its side-mounted engine driving the outside rear wheel was arguably so austere and unconventional that few customers were sufficiently courageous to sample its charms.

The tiny and fragile-looking Bond was the inspiration of Lancastrian Lawrie Bond who spent much of his early working career in the design offices of various companies including Atkinson & Co, Meadows Engineering and the Blackburn Aircraft Company. After World War Two Lawrie Bond established the Bond Aircraft and Engineering Company (Blackpool) Limited manufacturing aircraft and general vehicle parts under

Below: Attracting attention in the centre of Huddersfield the demure dimensions of the Bond Minicar make for an interesting comparison with its surroundings. With a top speed of 40mph and fuel economy approaching 100mpg, it is not surprising that this two-seater three wheeler was in demand. (Graham Hull, source unknown)

Above: This Bond was pictured in 1953 at the top of Countisbury Hill near Lynton in North Devon. When this photograph was taken the vehicle had completed 25,000 miles over a three year period. R.G.W.Burgess, the owner of the car, reported that his Bond had been virtually trouble-free; even the Perspex windscreen was as good as new and the ignition points were as supplied, not having required adjustment. (Author's collection)

government contract. When orders diminished he turned his attention to designing a small and inexpensive three wheeler which he had originally devised as a runabout for himself and his wife.

Like many of the minicars that emerged over the years, the Bond borrowed aircraft technology by using aluminium to keep weight as low as possible. Ease of maintenance was another requirement, along with simple and basic mechanical design. Power was derived from a Villiers 125cc two-stroke motorcycle engine built in unit with the gearbox and driving the single front wheel. There was no need for a separate chassis as the aluminium body formed the essential frame, and being an open car there was no provision for doors, the occupants merely stepped into it over the low sides. The Bond's austere specification did not allow for front wheel

Three Wheelers

Bond publicity material informed potential customers that the Minicar was light enough to be lifted by hand and therefore there was no need for a jack. Changing a rear wheel involved loosening the securing nuts before raising the side of the car and supporting it against one's thigh whilst replacing the offending wheel. There was no mention of what to do in the event of a front wheel puncture, or should an owner be unable to lift the car.
(National Motor Museum)

The Lancashire resort of Morecambe was host to Bond rallies in the early 1950s where this Mark A is seen preparing to compete along the seafront promenade. Over half a century later Bond enthusiasts maintain the tradition of meeting in this seaside town, only a few miles away from Preston where Bonds were manufactured.
(National Motor Museum)

braking, and the 10lb tyre inflation pressure provided rear suspension.

When Lawrie Bond designed his runabout he had little idea that his cars would be subjected to long-distance driving. So versatile was his Minicar that owners and enthusiasts were soon performing seemingly impossible feats of endurance including the Monte Carlo Rally. A motoring journalist braved the elements when he toured in one of the first Bonds for several thousand miles throughout the length and breadth of Europe.

Bond, without manufacturing resources, entrusted production to Sharps Commercials of Preston. Eventually Sharps bought out Lawrie Bond but retained his services on a consultancy basis.

Reliant, under the direction of Tom Williams, diversified from vans to motor cars and announced the Regal three-wheeler in the autumn of 1951. Unlike Bonds, Reliants were built with a box section pressed steel chassis with a water-cooled 747cc four-cylinder engine coupled to a four-speed gearbox driving the rear wheels. The engine was Reliant's own design and based on the Austin Seven engine. Pre-war, Austin had supplied engines to Reliant but when production was abandoned Tom Williams decided to manufacture his own units, taking this opportunity to improve on the original design.

The Regal became available in 1953 when it was produced in drophead form only. It had aluminium bodywork and although specified as a four-seater it was really better suited for two adults and a couple of children. Aluminium gave way to glass fibre with the introduction of the Regal Mk III in 1955 and all subsequent Reliants used this material.

What made three wheelers an attractive proposition was their relatively low running costs and not least the lower taxation. One of Reliant's marketing messages was that with only three wheels tyre costs were reduced!

At the end of 1951 Bond announced the Mark C Minicar with all-new styling that included dummy front wings. More curvaceous than the previous models, the wider frontal aspect of the car allowed the single wheel to be turned through ninety degrees thus negating any need for reverse gear. (Author's collection)

One of the most significant advantages as far as Bond and Reliant were concerned was that, in the UK, three

Three Wheelers

Motor car comfort at motor cycle cost

Using the same location as in the previous publicity photograph, the Bond Mark C has been turned around and the two children mysteriously dispensed with. Both pictures have an element of surrealism about them which gives them an eerie period feel. (Author's collection)

wheelers could be driven by holders of motorcycle licences.

Reliant three wheelers became a popular alternative for commercial use, and it wasn't only smaller businesses that appreciated their qualities. Such firms as Rolls-Royce, BOAC, the AA and various utilities all used them.

Reliants were also well-travelled and in addition to competing in the Monte Carlo Rally, they have, over the

years, made some remarkable treks to all corners of the world.

The forties and fifties were the golden age of post-war three wheelers, notwithstanding developments that heralded the bubblecar boom, and it was during this period that principal development was sustained. Certainly three-wheeling continued over successive decades offering a unique style of motoring, and this aspect of three wheels as opposed to four is discussed in a later chapter.

In 1953, at about the same time as Bond announced its Mark C model, Reliant Engineering introduced the Regal four-seater which was marketed as a convertible. The new model is seen at Earls Court in 1952 accompanied by the stalwart Regent van. Because of new cars being in short supply and petrol rationing, the aluminium-bodied three wheeler was the subject of widespread interest.
(Reliant publicity photograph, Author's collection)

Owning a car such as the Reliant Regal, the family could experience freedom and independence. Although austere in its appointment, it accommodated two adults and a couple of children to afford all that a four-wheeler could offer in the way of engineering, but with the benefits of reduced tax and running costs that three wheelers enjoyed. (Reliant publicity photograph Author's collection)

Introduced in 1951 the Fuldamobil owed its origins to caravan construction and featured leather clad plywood, although subsequent models had hammered aluminium panels. Known rather unkindly as the 'Silver Flea', Fuldamobils were sought after in their native Germany where motorists clamoured for even the most basic motorised transport. (National Motor Museum)

Three Wheelers

The Mark 2 Petite appeared in 1955 with several modifications including adoption of 12 inch wheels. It boasted car-like controls and was well appointed, the Villiers 28B engine affording 45mph top speed and 60mpg fuel consumption. This publicity photograph shows the Petite in its final form, production ceasing in 1958. (National Motor Museum)

AC was already a highly respected provider of sports cars when the firm diversified into economy car production in 1953 with the Petite Mark 1, an example seen undergoing restoration. These cars had an unusual wheel configuration, the two at the rear being 18 inches diameter and the single front being only 8 inches diameter. AC specified the rear-mounted Villiers 27B industrial single-cylinder engine to drive the rear wheels via triple v-belts connected to a Burman three-speed gearbox. (Author's collection)

Few AC Petites have survived but this example has been extensively restored and is pictured accompanied by a Trabant.
(Author's collection)

When it was introduced in 1954 the Gordon was advertised as being Britain's lowest priced three wheeler. Gordon Cars Ltd. was a subsidiary of Vernons Investments of Liverpool, the football pools promoter which was responsible for building and marketing Vi-Car invalid carriages. Vernons Investments can be applauded for exploiting the three wheeler minicar market, especially as the firm had experience building invalid carriages. Sadly, what embarked as being a good idea, failed rather miserably because the Gordon lacked a degree of sophistication with its crude drive mechanism and ultra-basic interior. Very few Gordons have survived and those that have are sought after and treasured by three wheeler enthusiasts. (Gordon Fitzgerald)

Gordons were not unlike early Reliants in styling. The engine was mounted at the side of the car beneath the driver with chain drive to the rear off-side wheel. When road tested by one of the motoring journals the reporter was less than enthusiastic towards the car's finish, not to mention gaps in the floor and wiring leads dangling from the fascia. (National Motor Museum)

Three Wheelers

Although the 'face' of the Gordon added to the car's rather comical stance, it was a highly competent machine. In 1955 a Gordon undertook a publicity test run between Lands End and John o' Groats and encouraging reports of the car's endeavours were penned by racing drivers SCH Davis and Pat Moss. (Gordon Fitzgerald)

A less than pretty Gordon as found in a garden at Southall in west London. It is clearly in a sorry state of decay but the engine appears to be intact.
(Gordon Fitzgerald)

Family motoring, Gordon style. Although spartanly attired, the Gordon offered economical motoring (courtesy of its 197cc engine), for two adults and a couple of small children. Gordons were simply constructed, the front wheel being suspended on Metalstick torsion bushes and the rear having flexible coil springs. The two-tone colour scheme signifies this is a de luxe model, and the maker's publicity material refers to it as being "Roomy, almost fool-proof and exceptionally well sprung to give you comfortable riding. (Gordon Fitzgerald)

The Gordon's unconventional engine and transmission layout, not to mention its austere appointment, led to relatively few sales during its three year production period. Is it surprising that despite their higher prices such cars as Bond and Reliant were more popular? (Author's collection)

Three Wheelers

The Mark II Reliant Regal was announced in 1955. It had slightly softer styling than its predecessor, a flat air intake and modified windscreen arrangement being evident. The car on the dias has an optional glass fibre hard top which afforded enhanced weather protection over the drop head model, and there was also a new Regal van to replace the Regent. The austere show surroundings are interesting compared to later events. (Reliant publicity photograph, Author's collection)

Glanfield Lawrence was a principal Reliant dealer with branches in London, Portsmouth, Bristol, Cardiff and Swansea. A Mark II Regal demonstrator with optional glass fibre hard top is pictured outside one of the company's branches, which happens to be an agent for other makes of economy car. (Author's collection)

Four adults aboard a Regal three wheeler made for some pretty cramped conditions, although Reliant advertised the Mark II as being a four-seater. This publicity photograph dating from 1955 depicts the subtle styling modifications which include trafficators fitted to the front wings immediately ahead of the doors. Before adoption of semaphores, drivers were obliged to make hand signals. (Reliant publicity photograph, Author's collection)

Reliant Regal 8cwt vans featured glass fibre bodywork which incorporated lightness with strength. This was one of the first applications of FRP - fibreglass reinforced plastic - and Fibreglass Limited of St.Helens in Lancashire combined with Reliant to produce this advertisement. (Author's collection)

Moulding the future...

Three wheels mean £5 tax instead of £12·10 if the van weighs less than 8 cwt. But . . . install a sturdy chassis, a 4-cylinder, water-cooled engine, a 4-speed and reverse gear box, a car-type rear axle with differential and 3 car size wheels — and what have you left for body weight! And come to that body *cost*! The bright answer is F.R.P. — as applied to this 5-cwt van by the Reliant Engineering Co. (Tamworth) Ltd. This tough little customer has a featherweight body with a heavyweight's strength. Its many curved panels, which would have cost a fortune to form by hand, were perfectly and simply moulded. There you have Fibreglass to the core!

Fibreglass have an advisory service which is expert, confidential and free.

FIBREGLASS
TRADE MARK

the backbone of Reinforced Plastics

CAR COMFORT FOR 5
at a total running cost of less than 1d. per mile

THE FAMILY SAFETY MODEL
Designed and Built for 2 adults and 3 children with full weather protection for all

SHARP'S COMMERCIALS LTD., (Est.

Left: The Bond Mark C Family Safety Model featured two occasional sideways facing rear seats that were suitable for small children. A less expensive model was classified as a three-seater on account of the manufacturer claiming three people could be accommodated (with difficulty) on the single bench seat. (Author's collection)

Left: With its hood in the raised position the Bond's passengers were assured of full weather protection. The vehicle depicted here is the Family Safety Model, the two occasional seats allowing the manufacturer to claim it as being a five-seater! (Author's collection)

Right: The spartan interior of the Mark C Bond. The standard model had a manually operated starter while that on the standard car was activated electrically. Note the single windscreen wiper, the column gear selector and minimal instrumentation. Unlike the previous models, Mark Cs had a single door on the passenger side of the vehicle. (Author's collection)

My word!
My BOND!

Mark C MODEL
(as illustrated)

THE OWNER OF A CAR is the best judge of its performance. A satisfied customer says: "I am really delighted
with the BOND MINICAR which I purchased from you. It
has all and more of the qualities I expected. Low upkeep
and running costs. So easy to manoeuvre and very comfortable.
Indeed, my word for value and economy is my **BOND**"

OTHER MODELS:
BOND MINITRUCK, BOND MINIVAN, Mark B
ALL FITTED WITH VILLIERS 197-c.c. ENGINE
Your car or motor cycle taken in part exchange
Immediate hire purchase acceptances

**SAFETY
SALOON**

The **BOND** *Minicar*

SEE IT - TRY IT - BUY IT *at* your London Distributors

SEE OUR
REPRESENTATIVE ON
STAND No. 20
1953 Cycle and Motor Cycle Show

★ Independent suspension
★ Brakes on all wheels
★ 180 degree steering
★ Cruising speed
40-45 m.p.h.
★ 80-90 m.p.g.
★ Exceptional weather
protection
★ £5 Road tax

Price of Mark C Model
£285
Inc. P.T. and Delivery

STOCKWELL RD.
LONDON, S.W.9
(Tel.: BRixton 6251) **PRIDE & CLARKE Ltd.** 237, BRIXTON HILL,
LONDON, S.W.2
(Tel.: TUlse Hill 3664)

The art of the illustrator made the Bond Minicar appear larger than it was. The proportions of the driver in relation to the car are exaggerated but nevertheless such artistry helped sell the product. Pride & Clarke were agents for a variety of three wheelers. During the era of austerity Bond Minicars enjoyed a popular following, such was the car's relatively low running costs and ease of maintenance. At £285 the Mark C Bond represented good value, especially when the recently introduced Austin A30 was priced at £497. Bonds were a familiar sight on Britain's roads, and agents like Pride & Clarke profited selling them on hire purchase with a deposit of around £90, the balance payable over 18 months. (Author's collection)

Three Wheelers

Left: This Mark C Bond was pictured with a bolt-on glass fibre hard top to provide improved weather protection. The car is a standard three-seater, hence the absence of the extended rear body section, and note the semaphore trafficator mounted on the windscreen. (Author's collection)

Left: This Mark C pictured outside the Silver City Air Ferry terminal in Kent in 1954 is a well travelled Bond. Lieutenant M Crosby and Captain T Mills drew much publicity through their unofficial entry in the Monte Carlo Rally by finishing the 2000 mile course. They started at Glasgow and followed the route taken by rally competitors and encountered few problems. Once they had completed the course they drove the 1000 or so miles home. (National Motor Museum)

Above: In Rome is Boanerges, Douglas Ferreira's Mark C Bond which he took on an extended tour of Europe in January 1956. He crossed the English Channel by Silver City Air Ferry, flying to Le Tourquet from Lydd. Douglas's route took him through France, Italy, Switzerland and Austria, covering 3546 miles in 19 days, much of it on atrocious roads. Apart from normal oiling, brake adjustment and attention to the silencer, the car required no attention. (Douglas Ferreira)

THE FAMILY SAFETY MODEL offers car comfort for four at a total running cost of less than 1d. per mile. Designed and built for two adults and two children with complete weather protection for all.

1957

THE SERVICE BEHIND THE NOW WELL ESTABLISHED BOND MINICAR ENSURES SECURITY

The Mark D Minicar was announced in May 1956 and featured a number of modifications over the Mark C. Similar in appearance to its predecessor, it was given a slightly different air intake grille and had longer rear wings on the Family Safety Model. Mechanically the improvements concerned the fitting of Villiers' 197cc 9E engine and, after 1957, adopting a four-speed gearbox in place of the three-speed unit. This publicity image confirms that the rear compartment really was only capable of accommodating two young children. (Author's collection)

Compare this Mark D with the photograph above. Being a Standard Model with a single bench seat it has the smaller rear wings. All Mark Ds had 12-volt electrics, which at least took some of the worry away from winter and night driving. (Author's collection)

TUL 84

The Bond's got everything! This publicity feature shows, clockwise, the Family Safety Model, the Hard Top Convertible Coupé, the rear compartment of the Family Model with its two sideways facing seats, and the front compartment with room for three abreast. (Author's collection)

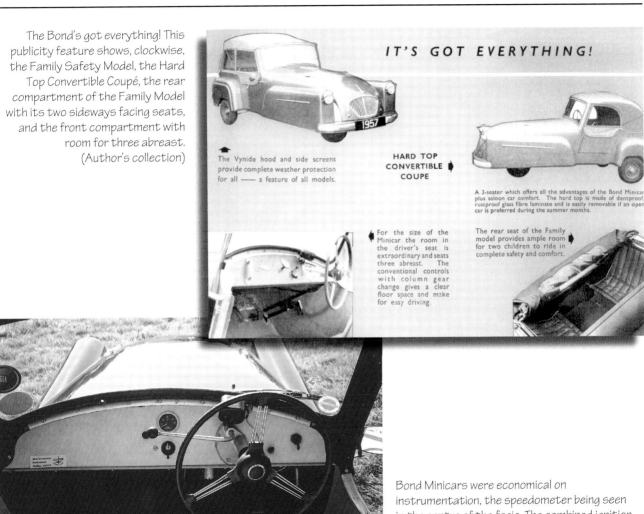

IT'S GOT EVERYTHING!

The Vynide hood and side screens provide complete weather protection for all — a feature of all models.

HARD TOP CONVERTIBLE COUPE

A 3-seater which offers all the advantages of the Bond Minicar plus saloon car comfort. The hard top is made of dentproof, rustproof glass fibre laminate and is easily removable if an open car is preferred during the summer months.

For the size of the Minicar the room in the driver's seat is extraordinary and seats three abreast. The conventional controls with column gear change gives a clear floor space and make for easy driving.

The rear seat of the Family model provides ample room for two children to ride in complete safety and comfort.

Bond Minicars were economical on instrumentation, the speedometer being seen in the centre of the facia. The combined ignition and electric starter is below it, and on the right of the steering wheel can be seen the direction indicator switch. The gear lever proved to be light and precise in use, thus effecting smooth gear changes. (Author's collection)

Three Wheelers

Among other manufacturers of three wheelers Bond was keen to attract motorcyclists as customers, and therefore marketed the Minicar to appeal to those who wanted greater sophistication than a combination outfit could offer. Note the obligatory pipe-smoking driver, always a good selling point! (Author's collection)

A brace of Mark D Bonds in good company. Alongside are a couple of later-type Minicars and in the background a number of Messerschmitts. (Author's collection)

Unusual means of transport for a unique motor car! Douglas Ferreira's Mark D Bond aboard a train headed by 4-4-2 *Synolda* at Ravenglass, the terminus of the Ravenglass & Eskdale Railway Company in Cumbria. The railway, which extends several miles inland to Boot village at the foot of Hard Knott, is a fifteen-inch gauge line which serves local residents as well as being a tourist attraction. When Douglas, who was once general manager of the railway, needed some welding to be carried out on his car, he sent it by train to the works' workshops. (Douglas Ferreira)

Three Wheelers

When the Reliant Regal Mark III was introduced for the 1956 model year it featured an all glass fibre body which minimised the number of joints required to produce this remarkably curvaceous shape. The hard top was a popular choice, and afforded superior weather protection to the coupé. The sliding windows helped the Regal to feel more like a 'proper' car: note the winking direction indicators replacing the semaphores. (Reliant publicity material, Author's collection)

In addition to the saloon, the coupé afforded open air motoring in the Reliant tradition which was popular with those motorists who had progressed from motorcycling. The fact that Regals now featured glass fibre bodywork panels attached to an ash frame afforded greater longevity than might otherwise have been maintained using steel. Free from rust was good for Reliant marketing. (National Motor Museum)

The Motor

December 11, 1957

RELIANT MK. III

Regal 3 wheel 4 seater
BIG CAR COMFORT-SMALL CAR ECONOMY

**THE SMALL CAR THAT HAS EVERYTHING
—APPEARANCE—PERFORMANCE—ECONOMY
—COMFORT—LESS TAX—LOWER INSURANCE**

The completely new fibre-glass body of the Regal Mk. III provides more room and more comfort for the four occupants. With a top speed of 65 m.p.h., the Regal cruises happily at 50 m.p.h. and can travel for 50 MILES on ONE GALLON of petrol with its 4-cylinder 750 c.c. engine. With normal car transmission and synchromesh gear box, the Regal Mk. III is the most up-to-date 3-wheeler in the Country.

Pay an early visit to your local dealer, he will be pleased to give you the fullest details.

"RELAX IN RELIANT!"

RELIANT ENGINEERING CO. (Tamworth) LTD.,
Two Gates, Tamworth, Staffs.

VAC 765

London Distributors: GLANFIELD LAWRENCE (HIGHBURY) LTD.,
Reliant House, 28/32 Highbury Corner, London, N.5

Big Car Comfort - Small Car Economy was Reliant's advertising message when marketing the Mark III Regal. With a top speed of 65mph, Regals cruised at 50mph and returned 50mpg which, in the mid-1950s represented value for money motoring. Although four-seaters, there was precious little space for rear-seat occupants, especially if they were tall. (Author's collection)

Three Wheelers

The sign of more affluent times? In the mid-1950s when two-car ownership was a rarity and reserved for the most wealthy, Reliant had no problem marketing the Regal as a second car for use by housewives taking children to school and doing family shopping. (Author's collection)

The NEW LOOK Regal Mk. 111.

THE IDEAL SECOND CAR

- Real economy at 50 MILES PER GALLON
- Max. Speed 65 m.p.h. cruising 50 m.p.h.
- Full Four-seater with luggage space behind rear seats.

Who takes your children to school? Who carries home that heavy shopping? Your wife, no doubt — but not in your car. Give her a second thought — buy a second car that will do 50 miles per gallon, cruise at 50 m.p.h. and yet costs only £5 per year in Tax. Very safe to drive and easy for parking. This is real motoring economy. This is The Reliant Regal Mk.III.

RELIANT RELIANT ENGINEERING CO. (TAMWORTH) LTD.
WATLING STREET, TWO GATES, TAMWORTH, STAFFS.

The interior of the Regal Mark III is more car-like than most other three wheelers, and the Smiths instrumentation is similar to that found on Austin A30/A35s. Because of the chassis layout the engine and gearbox seriously protruded into the cabin, and was intrusive in respect of space and noise. (Reliant publicity material, Author's collection)

This evocative piece of advertising is naively politically incorrect, before political correctness was ever thought about, of course. Marketing 'his and hers' cars, the Regal is obviously aimed at women motorists while the car in the background suggests a decidedly more masculine image.
(Author's collection)

26 April 1957

The Autocar

RELIANT

your second Car

MAKE YOUR FAMILY SELF-RELIANT

Who takes your children to school ? Who carries home that heavy shopping ? Your wife, no doubt — but not in your car. Give her a second thought — buy a second car that will do 50 miles per gallon, cruise at 50 m.p.h. and yet costs only £5 per year in Tax. Very safe to drive and easy for parking. This is real motoring economy. This is the Reliant Regal Mk. III.

50 to the GALLON — £5 TAX — LOW INSURANCE

RELIANT ENGINEERING CO. (Tamworth), LTD.
Dept. AC.I TWO GATES, TAMWORTH. STAFFS.
London Distributors: Glanfield Lawrence (Highbury) Ltd., Reliant House, 28-32 Highbury Corner, London, N.5

RELIANT "REGAL" Mk.III.

Making a debut in 1958, Reliant's Mark IV Regal was an updated version of the Mark III, and featured winding windows and separate direction indicators at the front. Wide-opening doors depict the easy access for both front and rear passengers, and the moulded fascia panel is evident, as are the utilitarian looking seats. Further evidence of economy is the fact that only a single windscreen wiper is deemed necessary. (Reliant publicity material, Author's collection)

Three Wheelers

Right: Reliant's stand at the 1958 Motor Cycle Show where at least six Mark IV vehicles are displayed, including a rolling chassis. When introduced, the Mark IV Regal cost £359 plus purchase tax which added a further £151, making it, apart from the Coronet which was £1 dearer, the most expensive three wheeler on the British market. There were several four wheelers that were cheaper, including the Ford Popular, the Frisky and the Goggomobil. (Reliant publicity material, Author's collection)

Left: The Mark V was only in production for a year when the Mark VI made its debut, combined sales of both models accounting for in excess of 13,000 vehicles. By now the latter's equipment included twin windscreen wipers and levels of comfort associated with many four wheelers of the period. Reliants enjoyed a popular following, not only from ex-motorcyclists but also families in search of a small and reliable family saloon with low running and depreciation costs. (Reliant publicity material, Author's collection)

The architect of a number of three wheeler designs during the Fifties was David Gottlieb who, in addition to penning the Allard Clipper, styled the Coronet and Powerdrive. When Allard abandoned Clipper production after disappointing sales, Gottlieb produced the Powerdrive which was stylishly modern and accommodated three abreast on the bench seat. Being nearly twelve feet in length it was no minicar, but it was light in weight courtesy of its aluminium construction.
(Author's collection)

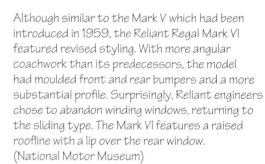

Although similar to the Mark V which had been introduced in 1959, the Reliant Regal Mark VI featured revised styling. With more angular coachwork than its predecessors, the model had moulded front and rear bumpers and a more substantial profile. Surprisingly, Reliant engineers chose to abandon winding windows, returning to the sliding type. The Mark VI features a raised roofline with a lip over the rear window.
(National Motor Museum)

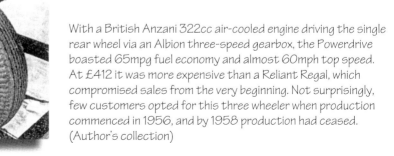

With a British Anzani 322cc air-cooled engine driving the single rear wheel via an Albion three-speed gearbox, the Powerdrive boasted 65mpg fuel economy and almost 60mph top speed. At £412 it was more expensive than a Reliant Regal, which compromised sales from the very beginning. Not surprisingly, few customers opted for this three wheeler when production commenced in 1956, and by 1958 production had ceased.
(Author's collection)

The Bubble Boom

Small but perfectly formed' is one way of describing the bubblecars which emerged to satisfy a particular demand during the 1950s and '60s. Mainly three wheelers, bubblecars offered a unique aspect to minimal motoring and because of their unusual design they mostly escaped the stigmas associated with economy cars.

Cheeky and delightfully charismatic as they now appear, the concept behind the bubblecar has been largely overlooked. Whereas three wheelers such as Bonds and Reliants evoked curiosity and were seen as economy cars serving as motoring on a shoestring, the bubblecar is viewed as being enchanting and adding to the rich tapestry of automotive history.

Because bubblecars appeared so impractical they have engendered a loyal following throughout the world. Greeted with acclaim and summoning inverted snobbery, they have attracted cult and celebrity status. Egg-shaped, bubblecars were more akin to motor scooters than motorcars and yet they provided a means of comfort and sophistication that was denied to

The style of the Isetta was modified throughout its production. These early models, in the course of production, show the finishing process being applied. As in the previous picture these are four wheeled models, the three wheeler having yet to be introduced. (BMW)

Above: Bubblecars in the making. Produced with usual BMW efficiency Isettas found a level of popularity they failed to secure when manufactured in Italy by Iso. BMW acquired the rights to build Isettas when Eberhard Wolff saw the bubblecar exhibited at the Geneva Motor Show in March 1954. Iso was looking to sell Isetta, which went into production in 1953 and BMW was in need of a small car to market in Germany. Originally a four wheeler with a very narrow rear track to obviate the need for a differential, the design was changed to a three wheeler to benefit from lower taxation in certain countries. (BMW)

In 1956, the first full year of German production, BMW built more than 22,000 Isettas, this being the 10,000th. This was the year when three wheelers were first produced. (BMW)

scooterists or motorcyclists.

The bubblecar concept was conceived in France during World War Two when architect Paul Arzens needed to travel around Paris. A petrol-engined car being out of the question, he devised the *l'Oeuf-Electrique* - the Electric Egg - in 1942. Driven by an electric motor powered by five 250amp batteries, Arzens managed a respectable 45mph and a range of up to 60 miles.

A little over a decade later Renzo Rivolta introduced the modern bubble in the form of the Isetta. The Isettas, designed by Ermenegildo Preti and built in Milan by Rivolta's Isotherm refrigerator manufacturing business, were initially deprived of the success they deserved. Italian motorists, more accustomed to the Fiat Toppolino, were suspicious of this little wonder which opened at the front swallowing its passengers. It was only when BMW acquired a license to manufacture Isettas that they were bought in substantial numbers by Germans who had previously been denied affordable transport after the war.

The first Isettas were four wheelers, with the rear wheels close together to avoid having to fit a differential. The 236cc air-cooled twin-cylinder engine sat above the rear axle producing a maximum speed approaching 45mph. Even when driven hard it was possible to achieve

The 50,000th Isetta to come off the production line. The plate on the front of the car tells us that it is a 300 model, a three wheeler destined for export. Note the two-tone colour scheme and the pod-type headlamps fitted into elongated nacelles above the front wings. (BMW)

Three Wheelers

Isettas were equipped with sun roofs which, it has been claimed, allowed a means of exiting the car in the event of the single front door being damaged and inoperable. Because of the large glass area and confined space within the cabin, driving in hot sunny weather proved uncomfortable, which is why the opening roof is useful.
(Author's collection)

Pictured at an enthusiasts' rally this late model Isetta has right hand drive. The driver and the engine are positioned on the same side of the car which caused stability problems. So that the car would not overturn on right hand bends and corners, Isetta engineers devised a method of installing ballast. When unsuspecting owners removed the metal weight from the left hand side of the car, difficulties in maintaining equilibrium were encountered.
(Author's collection)

The Isetta's drive train includes a 298cc air-cooled single-cylinder BMW engine (here partly dismantled). The four-speed gearbox affords a top speed of around 50mph and petrol consumption in the region of 66mpg. Unlike some three wheelers the Isetta featured a reverse gear and hydraulic braking on all wheels. (Author's collection)

50mpg. The main problem with four-wheelers was that in certain countries, Britain included, they attracted full taxation. When BMW introduced a three-wheeled Isetta its popularity immediately increased.

Anyone who has ridden in a bubblecar will appreciate the technique of getting in and out through the single front door. Perfect for driving in congested cities, bubbles can be parked sideways to take up less space and for occupants to alight on the pavement.

Of similar concept is the Heinkel which was built in Germany by the famous aeroplane maker. Post-war restrictions imposed upon German aircraft manufacturers prevented them from building military

equipment and diversification into motor production was one way of remaining in business. Unlike BMWs, which featured a separate chassis, Heinkels were designed with unitary construction which made them lighter and more aerodynamic.

Heinkels were produced as three and four-wheelers and as well as being built in Germany were also assembled in Ireland and later in England by Trojan. When Isettas were built in a redundant railway locomotive works at Brighton, they were the only vehicles to be manufactured in a factory that was without road access, all materials and finished cars being delivered by train!

The Isetta's single front door formed the front panel of the car. Entry to the vehicle interior was made all the easier as the steering column was attached to the door and swivelled out of the way. The inside was surprisingly spacious and comfortable. Adjacent to the Isetta 300 is a 600, a much larger four-wheeler which in addition to its front opening door has a single side door access to the rear seats. (Author's collection)

The styling arrangement on this Brighton-built Isetta dates from 1958 when sliding windows became part of the 'export' specification. Modifications to the car's suspension resulted in a softer ride. British made Isettas were built at Brighton in a disused railway locomotive works which were converted to car production. All components were delivered to the factory by train and finished cars left by the same method as there was no road access. (Author's collection)

Three Wheelers

Continuing the bubble concept Heinkels were introduced in March 1956, by which time BMW-built Isettas were available. That Heinkels and Isettas shared styling similarities is obvious, and Heinkel even went as far as negotiating with BMW so as not to infringe any styling and manufacturing patents. Close inspection reveals a number of differences between the two designs, Heinkel having adopted unitary construction for his cars to limit weight. While Heinkels employed a single door in Isetta fashion, they were four-seaters, the front seat folding to allow access to the narrow rear bench which was suitable for children or carrying luggage. Note the Morris Minor van in the background. (Author's collection)

As the name implies Messerschmitts were also built by a famous German aircraft manufacturer. Messerschmitt, like, Heinkel, faced restrictions and building cars provided work and fulfilled a need for German motorists. Despite their association with aircraft manufacturing neither Heinkels nor Messerschmitts owed their origins to aeronautics, and any notions about Messerschmitts being built from superfluous aircraft components can be firmly discounted.

Arguably Messerschmitts had the most distinctive profile of all the bubbles. They were aerodynamically shaped with room for a couple of occupants confined to sitting in tandem beneath a Plexiglass canopy and lived up to their Kabinenroller (cabin scooter) name. A journalist described passengers ensconced in a Messerschmitt as, 'People in aspic'.

In addition to Isettas, Heinkels and Messerschmitts there emerged a number of designs, some more successful than others. The Peel, a diminutive single seater, materialised from the Isle of Man but was more at home on its native narrow lanes than on the mainland's highways. Fitted with a handle that served as a reversing aid, this was the smallest car made in the United Kingdom.

Appearing somewhat top-heavy the minimalist pear-shaped Scootacar that was built in Leeds by Hunslet, the railway locomotive firm, attracted few customers.

During the Suez Crisis and the ensuing fuel shortages bubblecars became a familiar and welcome sight providing essential and economical transport for thousands of people. By the end of the 1950s the bubble boom was in decline: plentiful petrol supplies, increasing prosperity and technical developments brought new and exciting designs including the Mini. Although bubblecars were consigned to history by the mid '60s it is fortunate that examples have survived to become collectable classics.

In addition to being built in Germany, Heinkels were manufactured in the Irish Republic by Dundalk Engineering. To distinguish the Dundalk cars from their German-made cousins they were known as Heinkel Is and carried a small letter I following the Heinkel's winged H emblem. This example has seen better days and requires extensive renovation before being roadworthy. The decline of bubblecars in the 1960s led to numerous vehicles being scrapped. (Author's collection)

for sale !
1958 **Heinkel** - rare Irish model, low mileage, easy restoration, needs welding for mot. s/roof, fsh, poss p/x sensible offers - no traders

Three Wheelers

Cruise twenty miles a day for a shilling! This was Trojan's claim when it adopted production of the Heinkel which boasted fuel economy of 95mpg. A shilling is equivalent to five pence, and in 1962 a gallon of petrol cost around five shillings, 25p. It was possible to drive more than 300 miles on a tank full of petrol, a fill-up costing around eighteen shillings or 90p. According to Trojan publicity, driving 10,000 miles a year would cost in the region of £26 including oil consumption. (Trojan publicity material, Author's collection)

Above: When Dundalk Engineering abandoned Heinkel assembly in 1962, production was transferred to Trojan of Purley Way in Croydon. Trojans had enjoyed a loyal following since 1922 and in post-war years the Type 15 van was a familiar sight on Britain's streets delivering provisions to shops. Croydon-built Heinkels were sold as the Trojan 200 in four model variations, 601 and 603 being three wheelers, right and left hand drive respectively, 602 and 604 being four wheelers. This model 603 is pictured in company with a vintage four-seater tourer which was sold with solid tyres, although pneumatics were available at an additional cost of £5. (Author's collection)

Sixties' fashions are evident in this publicity photograph used by Trojan to depict the virtues of its Model 200 bubblecar. Having ample power to spare whether driving on the flat or climbing the steepest mountain passes was the message, but why the manufacturer deemed it appropriate to feature its three wheeler alongside a horse remains unclear. (Trojan publicity material, Author's collection)

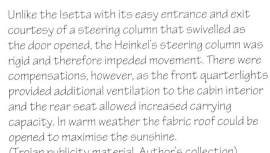

Unlike the Isetta with its easy entrance and exit courtesy of a steering column that swivelled as the door opened, the Heinkel's steering column was rigid and therefore impeded movement. There were compensations, however, as the front quarterlights provided additional ventilation to the cabin interior and the rear seat allowed increased carrying capacity. In warm weather the fabric roof could be opened to maximise the sunshine.
(Trojan publicity material, Author's collection)

Three Wheelers

The Trojan's manoeuvrability gave it a turning circle that was tighter than that of a London taxi. This specially prepared publicity photograph says it all, the parking space being no more than 10 feet long. (Trojan publicity material, Author's collection)

Below: Although both cars depicted have left hand drive with the doors hinged on the right so as to allow easiest entry and exit, the doors were not reverse-hinged on right hand drive models. With their rigid steering columns, RHD Trojans compromised the ease of entry and exit which drivers and passengers of LHD cars had come to expect. (Trojan publicity material, Author's collection)

Above: Both 601 and 603 Trojan models are featured here, each having 198cc single-cylinder 4-stroke engines, developing 10bhp at 5500rpm, and with four-speed transmissions. Specifications include independent suspension at the front with leading swing arms incorporating coil springs and heavy duty shock absorbers, and a big trailing swing arm at the rear with a hydraulically damped telescopic shock absorber. Brakes were hydraulic at the front and cable operated by hand at the rear. Many bubblecar enthusiasts prefer Heinkel and Trojans to Isettas because of their low centre of gravity and the free-running engines. Production of Trojans at Croydon continued until 1964 by which time demand had dwindled to the extent that the operation was unprofitable. (Author's collection)

Three Wheelers

This recently taken photograph of an early Messerschmitt illustrates the very narrow tub in which the occupants are confined. The rear passenger sits with their legs parallel to the driver's. (Author's collection)

The Messerschmitt was highly acclaimed when it made its debut in March 1953 at the Geneva Motor Show. Despite its name being associated with aeroplane manufacture, the Messerschmitt's evolution owed nothing to aviation. Its origins can be traced to invalid carriage design and efforts by designer Fritz Fend to provide a means of inexpensive transportation for the war wounded. Fend was unable to finance the project, which evolved from hand-propelled machines to petrol-engined cabin scooters. In Professor Willy Messerschmitt he found a willing collaborator who, like Ernst Heinkel, had been prohibited from building military aircraft. (Author's collection)

Above: In 1955 a more powerful KR200 Messerschmitt was introduced with a Fichtel & Sachs 191cc single-cylinder two-stroke engine. Cosmetic modifications included a restyled Plexiglas dome, a wrap-around windscreen and redesigned front wings which enabled the vehicle to have a wider track. It was the shape of the dome and the fact that the car's occupants sat in tandem that added to the misconception that Messerschmitts were built out of surplus aircraft components! (Author's collection)

Above: The dimensions of the Messerschmitt Kabinenroller can be gauged from this photograph taken in the 1950s. With room for two passengers sitting in tandem, Messerschmitts featured handlebar steering, twist-grip throttle and a hinged Plexiglass dome which, when raised, allowed easy access to the vehicle's interior. On all models domes are hinged on the right of the tub which means that occupants step from the car into the road where driving is on the right. Where vehicles drive on the left, care has to be taken not to open the dome in the path of on-coming traffic. Early Messerschmitts had 174cc Fichtel & Sachs single-cylinder engines: thus the KR 175 model designation. Despite similarities with motorcycles the clutch and brake controls were car-like, and on the driver's left was the gear selector. The handbrake was positioned on the driver's right, and on early models windscreen wipers were manually operated, which made heavy rain conditions rather trying. Within a few months the wipers were electrically activated. (Author's collection)

Three Wheelers

Below: Messerschmitt's United Kingdom concessionaires made no apology for marketing the Cabin Scooter to the motorcycling fraternity. What is not mentioned here is that during hot sunny weather the Messerschmitt's interior became very uncomfortable, and even a sliding hatch in the dome gave little relief. For those more used to motorcycling, Messerschmitts did indeed provide an economic level of comfort and refinement that was previously unknown. (Author's collection)

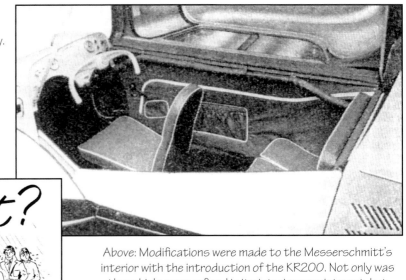

Above: Modifications were made to the Messerschmitt's interior with the introduction of the KR200. Not only was the vehicle more refined in its interior appointment, but rear seating was arranged so that a young child could be accommodated alongside an adult. The split seat was made to fold to accommodate luggage, and to extend the Messerschmitt's carrying capacity a rack could be fitted above the engine cover. The handlebar steering was also modified to be less representative of a motorcycle. (Author's collection)

Messerschmitts were marketed in America with some success. In the land of plenty where fuel costs were minimal and motorists were more used to seeing huge motor cars with gas-guzzling engines, they were the subject of curiosity. This KR200 complete with American specification nudge bars front and rear is pictured in Arizona. In addition to the saloon, roadster, cabrio-limousine, and sport versions were available, this being the cabrio-limousine with the fabric roof removed. The roadster was equipped with a hood while the sport featured a rigid body, a Plexiglass sports windshield and a tonneau cover extending over both seats.
(Gordon Fitzgerald)

The Messerschmitt's drive train showing the 191cc single-cylinder Fichtel & Sachs engine; the spare wheel fits aft of the fuel tank and is fitted to the underside of the engine cover. A contemporary road test report was not entirely complimentary when discussing the Messerschmitt's virtues: "It has 2½ seats; the driver has a central one to himself and at the back there is a bench which will hold a small wife and child, or a larger wife and a shopping basket, or again, a brother and his medium-sized dog." Hardly politically correct! (Author's collection)

Three Wheelers

A gaggle of Messerschmitts at an enthusiasts' rally showing a variety of models. In the mid-1950s Messerschmitt returned to aircraft manufacturing and in so doing sold the rights to produce bubblecars to FMR. Fahrzeug und Maschinebau Gmbh Regensburg continued production using the Messerschmitt name but in time a new emblem was adopted incorporating the FMR initials within linked diamonds. Problems had arisen when Daimler-Benz objected to the use of the Messerschmitt 'Eagle' design which it claimed was too much like the Mercedes three-pointed star. FMR then designed a new logo with the letters in linked circles, which annoyed Auto-Union who considered the design too much akin to its own. (Author's collection)

Fritz Fend subjected his Cabin-Scooter to endurance testing at Hockenheim on 29th August 1955. His aim was to keep the vehicle running for twenty-fours courtesy of a team of six drivers, an achievement that shattered many records. The car used for the record attempt was one specially designed with a wind-cheating body, and along the straights it reached in excess of 77mph. Overall, the results were 65.754mph over 1000 miles, 65.24mph over 2000km, and 64.03mph average throughout the twenty-four hours. It is pictured here passing a signalling post during practice runs at Hockenheim ahead of the endurance attempt, the plus sign and downward pointing arrow indicating that all is well. (Author's collection)

The bubblecar era was responsible for a number of remarkable designs including the Scootacar which was built in Leeds by Hunslet, better known for its railway engines. The Scootacar was designed by Henry Brown, no stranger to motor vehicles, having previously produced the ill-fated Rodley car which attracted the dubious nomination for the worst car on the market. Scootacars never achieved the popularity of Isettas, Trojans and Messerschmitts, but they did provide economical motoring for around a thousand customers. (Author's collection)

In similar fashion to Messerschmitts Scootacars employed handlebar steering. There is room for two passengers sitting in tandem on the uncomfortable looking seat that masked the air-cooled engine and which deterred most people from undertaking lengthy journeys. According to contemporary road test reports there was little space for luggage or shopping, and suspension was somewhat rigid. (Author's collection)

Three Wheelers

This forlorn looking Scootacar was discovered by bubblecar enthusiast Gordon Fitzgerald in the 1970s. The glass fibre body was made in two halves, the join being made along the top and down the front and rear. By having the engine beneath the driver's seat it was possible to maintain minimal vehicle dimensions. While the windscreen was made from safety glass all other glazed areas were formed from Perspex. On the car pictured the spare wheel which is normally carried at the rear is missing. (Gordon Fitzgerald)

Unkind words were attributed to the Scootacar when it was introduced in the autumn of 1957. Said to resemble a mobile telephone box, at £275 it was the cheapest enclosed car on the British market and its economy promised both a spartan interior and frugal petrol consumption of around 80mpg. The Scootacar's body was mounted on a steel platform to which the sliding pillar and coil-spring front and swinging-arm rear suspension were grafted. The reliable 197cc Villiers single-cylinder two-stroke promised 40mph, although a cruising speed of 30mph was more comfortable. (Author's collection)

Right: Eugene Chung with his P50 pictured outside the hospital where he practised as a surgeon in the 1960s. The vehicle's tiny dimensions are evident, and it goes without saying that Peels were better suited for the rural lanes of the Isle of Man where they were manufactured by Peel Engineering, a plastics company specialising in motor boat hulls.
(Gordon Fitzgerald)

Above: Another bubble oddity is the Peel, the most diminutive car built in the United Kingdom. The prototype machine featured a single wheel at the front but, following testing, the configuration was reversed. When the Peel P50 first appeared in 1962 the bubblecar era was virtually over, but priced at a little under £200 it nevertheless attracted some customers. Around 50 P50s were made, each fitted with a 49cc DKW fan-cooled two-stroke which afforded a breathtaking 40mph.
(Gordon Fitzgerald)

Left: With its Cyclops headlamp and single door, the proportions of the Peel make for claustrophobia. There was no necessity for Peels to have a reverse gear, especially when a handle attached to the rear of the car gave it manoeuvrability.
(Author's collection)

Three Wheelers

Above: Driving a Peel on British roads today can be a daunting experience. Gordon Fitzgerald, the owner of this example, ventures only short distances because top speed and lethargic acceleration, not to mention dwarfish size, can prove hazardous on busy routes, especially with fast moving heavy lorries around. (Author's collection)

Above: In 1965 Peel introduced the Trident which was marketed as a refined version of the P50. The DKW engine was retained, but at the rear of the car. Tridents were built in two sections, the lower being a moulded plastic unit attached to a steel platform, the upper an acrylic bubble. Slightly larger than P50s, Tridents were two-seaters. (Gordon Fitzgerald)

Above: Introduced in 1983, the Alan Evans Bamby bubblecar incorporated a 49cc engine mated to a three-speed automatic transmission, and had hydraulic braking on the front wheels. Like the Peel it was a single-seater, which at 107kg, was sufficiently light to be manoeuvred by hand. The car's performance was negligible, however, its redeeming feature being 100mpg economy. At £1389 plus tax it was excessively priced and few were sold. Production ceased in 1985 after around 50 examples were built. (Gordon Fitzgerald)

Decline and Revival

The popularity of three wheelers declined in the early 1960s mainly as a result of the introduction of innovative and inexpensive small cars. Spearheading technology was the Mini which, with its promise of fun, was as much a fashion statement as a purposeful means of transport.

represented full-size motoring on four wheels, making bubblecars obsolete.

The true economy car was salvation when manufacturing and fuel shortages had restricted car ownership at the end of World War Two, and again in the mid-Fifties with the onset of the Suez Crisis.

In December 1956, Bond announced the Mark E Minicar which, under its modern skin largely featured the Mark D's technology. A healthy demand for Mark Ds convinced Bond management to defer putting the new model into production for a year, but when it was time to commence building problems became apparent. The car handled badly, threatening to overturn whilst cornering, which prompted a re-evaluation of the chassis design to reduce the wheelbase and widen the rear track. (National Motor Museum)

The arrival of the Mini in 1959 put an end to post-war austerity. Instead of queuing for rationed goods with coupons at the ready, motorists lined up to buy the car that consigned everything before it to history. Minis

Nevertheless, there were those who were ready to declare three wheelers dead, to ridicule their very existence ridding the streets of tripodal antiquities.

For all the new and exciting designs that emerged

Three Wheelers

The Mark E's modern lines are evident in this publicity photograph released before the car went into production in January 1958. Having a door either side of the car was a welcome feature but the car's design and construction were responsible for it being heavier than its predecessor. The 197cc Villiers engine was hard put to afford adequate performance, the problem being resolved by increasing the engine size. (National Motor Museum)

The Mark F makes for an interesting comparison with the Riley alongside it. While the Riley was stylish and afforded comfort together with performance expected of a sports saloon, the Bond was utilitarian and provided basic accommodation. Its running costs, compared to that of the Riley, were minimal. (Author's collection)

Left: Within a year of the Mark E going into production, Bond introduced the Mark F with the Villiers 246cc engine. The car pictured is Douglas Ferreira's demonstrator at Tarn Hows in the Lake District, the two ladies being members of Bond's sales team. Douglas was appointed the company's sole sales representative at Bond director Colonel Gray's invitation, following his treks across Europe in his Bond three wheelers. In 1959, Douglas Ferreira made history when he drove his Mark F from Lands End to John o' Groats in under twenty-four hours. Keeping to a schedule which meant averaging 37mph, he reached his destination with twenty minutes to spare. (Douglas Ferreira)

in the early Sixties there remained, nevertheless, a demand, albeit somewhat diminished, for economy cars from a clientele far more accustomed to driving on three wheels than four. Despite increasing prosperity it wasn't everyone that was happy to forego minimal motoring, even if it did mean sacrificing an element of comfort and refinement.

Despite the Mini's arrival bursting the bubble boom, both Reliant and Bond survived in the hands of motorists appreciative of the often veiled virtues of family three wheelers. Neither manufacturer buried its head in the sand; new models kept pace with technology, but even

Three Wheelers

The Mark F proved popular and accounted for around one hundred cars a week leaving the Preston factory. Seen at a classic car event, this example provides plenty of fun for three adults and a trio of children. (Author's collection)

A Mark F in the company of a Mark D tourer. The differences in styling between the models is clearly evident, many enthusiasts preferring the rounded contours of the early models to the later more angular types. In the background can be seen a Messerschmitt and an Isetta. (Author's collection)

Bond introduced a number of body configurations for its Minicars, and saloons were particularly sought after as they afforded a degree of comfort and refinement without compromising the marque's ethos. The arrival of the Mini in 1959 had considerable impact on Bonds and Reliants and, in order to sustain sales, manufacturers constantly updated model specification to remain attractive. This Mark G saloon is in splendid condition and demonstrates how far Bond design had changed since the introduction of the Mark A. (Author's collection)

so, by the late 1960s the three wheeler market could no longer sustain two major companies. Reliant acquired Bond Cars in 1969 by which time the latter had launched the 875, an all-new car designed to rival the Regal. Tamworth's offering was more car-like than ever with its modern shape and reverse-angled rear window as seen on the Ford Anglia.

Partly because Reliant had cornered the market, and partly because Bond experienced production difficulties, the 875 never enjoyed the popularity it deserved. What should have been a refined and proficient machine, with its Hillman Imp engine, was pared down to extreme basics in the search for economy. When Reliant closed the Bond factory there were cries of indignation: Bond wasn't dead though, and out of the ashes rose the Bond Bug, a Reliant designed and built eccentricity that has since achieved cult status.

Against all odds and numerous changes of ownership Reliant survived the millennium and this classic remained in production and was built under licence in Dorset by B&N Engineering until 2003 when production was halted because of design and technical difficulties.

Three Wheelers

The 250G's 246cc single-cylinder Villiers Mk35A engine and transmission fitted ahead of the front wheel gave adequate performance. When a twin-cylinder 249cc engine became available in 1963 it pushed the car's performance to 60mph. (Author's collection)

The Bond 250G was styled so that windscreen pillars were moved forwards and the rear screen inverted in Ford Anglia and Citroën Ami 6 fashion. With winding windows, padded door interiors and a rear seat wide enough to accommodate four children, the vehicle was both relatively sophisticated and functional. (National Motor Museum)

In the 1970s and '80s with fuel costs spiralling, the three wheeler concept was given a renewed lease of life. A myriad of microcars emerged, mainly from France, to fulfil the search for true economy. Minimal motoring surfaced in the form of often peculiar machines once epitomized by Peels and Scootacars. Met with little enthusiasm in Britain these achieved considerable following in mainland Europe where tax and driving concessions assured their proliferation.

More in the Morgan image, such cars as the Berkeley and Coronet were well received confirming that three wheels did not necessarily compromise performance. The essence of the Morgan was again captured in the seventies: for a modest outlay it was possible to enjoy all the thrills of a bygone era but with all the advantages of modern technology. The recipe for such fulfilment were kit cars that employed donor chassis re-engineered with trailing rear wheels and accommodating lightweight bodies in Morganesque fashion. Citroën's 2CV, with its exposed air-cooled flat-twin engine served the purpose: garnish it with aero screens, don goggles and flying helmet and experience budget three wheeling.

Modern three wheelers satisfy a demand for inexpensive yet reliable and multi-functional commercial use. Many will recall the Scammell 'Scarab' mechanical horses that were to be seen at many railway stations and goods yards in the early post-war era, and Reliant successfully marketed the Ant abroad. Now a new generation of micro three wheelers, emanating from Italy and France, are keeping pace with demand.

So what does the future promise for three wheelers? When companies such as Volkswagen are promoting their 1-Litre prototype car the outlook must be good. With its 0.3 litre single-cylinder diesel engine capable of propelling the machine at speeds of up to 120km/h and using only a litre of fuel per 100 kilometres, three wheels bode well.

Three Wheelers

The Regal 3/25 was sold as a commercial variant, the model shown here being the 3/25 Supervan. Advertising a storage and removals company, the vehicle is certainly eye-catching, but isn't there something just faintly familiar about it? No doubt *Trotter's Independent Trading Company* would be impressed ... (Author's collection)

Bond announced a completely new three wheeler in 1965. This was the Hillman Imp-powered 875 with its engine in the tail to provide terrific performance. The 875's extensive testing halted production until June 1966. The 875 made a name for itself when John Surtees took a prototype around Brands Hatch at speeds approaching 100mph! With such potential Bond decided to reduce power and fit the low compression Imp engine, which still released an athletic 80mph and fuel consumption of 50mpg. Despite the 875's attractive lines it did not sell as hoped and even a face-lift failed to improve matters. (National Motor Museum)

Styling is everything! Reliant introduced the Robin (the concept created by Ogle Design which was responsible for the Scimitar sports saloon), in 1974. Ultra-modern in appearance, Robins were well received and diverted to some extent from the three wheeler image. Photographed at a publicity launch at Goodwood, Robins take to the circuit in the hands of motoring journalists. (Reliant publicity material, Author's collection)

Reliant marketed the Robin to be desirable to younger families as well as traditional customers. Certainly the Ogle styling was attractive and, with features including a hatchback, appeal was enhanced.
(Reliant publicity material, Author's collection)

Three Wheelers

By the 1970s there was insufficient demand for three wheelers to sustain both Reliant and Bond. The outcome was that Reliant bought Bond and closed the Preston factory. The Bond name was retained for this wedge-shaped cutie, the Bond Bug, which quickly realised cult status, and of the 2270 built a number have survived to be revered by enthusiasts.
(National Motor Museum)

The Ant, which was intended for export, is a Reliant rarity. Some were sold on the home market and a number were built in Greece. Ants served many practical uses, from pick-ups to tippers, milk floats to road sweepers, production accounting for 1888 vehicles. (Author's collection)

Bond Bugs were officially available in a single colour - Bug Tangerine. Surviving examples have often been repainted, and a collection of them are seen here with a Reliant Rialto, the model that succeeded the Robin in 1982. (Author's collection)

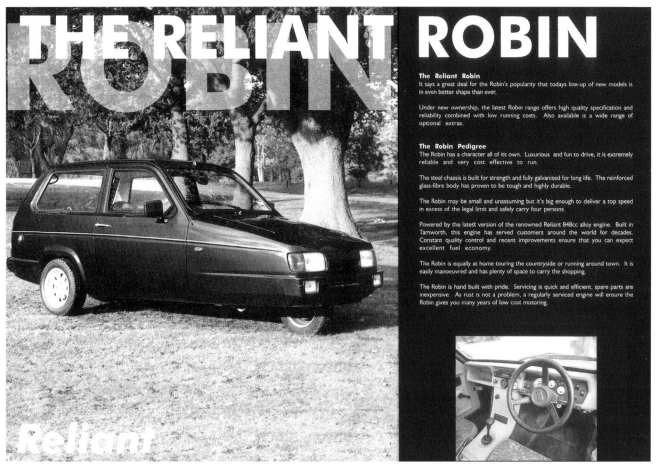

THE RELIANT ROBIN

The Reliant Robin

It says a great deal for the Robin's popularity that todays line-up of new models is in even better shape than ever.

Under new ownership, the latest Robin range offers high quality specification and reliability combined with low running costs. Also available is a wide range of optional extras.

The Robin Pedigree

The Robin has a character all of its own. Luxurious and fun to drive, it is extremely reliable and very cost effective to run.

The steel chassis is built for strength and fully galvanised for long life. The reinforced glass-fibre body has proven to be tough and highly durable.

The Robin may be small and unassuming but it's big enough to deliver a top speed in excess of the legal limit and safely carry four persons.

Powered by the latest version of the renowned Reliant 848cc alloy engine. Built in Tamworth, this engine has served customers around the world for decades. Constant quality control and recent improvements ensure that you can expect excellent fuel economy.

The Robin is equally at home touring the countryside or running around town. It is easily manoeuvred and has plenty of space to carry the shopping.

The Robin is hand built with pride. Servicing is quick and efficient, spare parts are inexpensive. As rust is not a problem, a regularly serviced engine will ensure the Robin gives you many years of low cost motoring.

In 1989, demand for Reliant three wheelers summoned the re-introduction of the Robin, albeit in an updated guise. Built as a hatchback, it was as popular with families as it was with traders wanting a durable vehicle with minimal running costs. (Reliant publicity material, Author's collection)

The Robin was restyled in 1995 to make it all the more attractive. When Reliant decided to abandon Robin production in 2000, assembly was transferred to B&N Engineering in Dorset where they were manufactured to order, around ten vehicles a week, until 2003. Owing to technical difficulties production was halted for an unspecified period. (Author's collection)

Popular with business people, Reliants are put to a variety of uses. An advocate of the marque, this window cleaner has owned a variety of models and appreciates their reliability and low running costs. (Author's collection)

Three Wheelers

Modern styling was the key to the Robin when it was updated in 1995. Subtle curves and the employment of Vauxhall Corsa headlamps helped maintain a modern appearance. (Author's collection)

Lawrie Bond and Berkeley Caravans of Biggleswade combined their talents to produce the Berkeley three wheeler in prototype form in 1956. Berkeley was one of the largest producers of caravans in the United Kingdom, and its innovative construction methods, together with Bond's engineering expertise, produced this handsome three wheeler. (National Motor Museum)

Compared to some three wheelers, Berkeleys offered deft styling and performance. Top speed, courtesy of the Excelsior 328cc engine, was 60mph. In recent years Berkeley enthusiasts have been able to acquire new bodyshells for their cars and have replaced original engines with a variety of units to include those from the Mini and air-cooled twin-cylinder Citroëns. (Author's collection)

Three Wheelers

Frisky three wheelers were marketed as the Family Three and were advertised as being four-seaters. Suicide doors with leading edges immediately above the front wheels suggest that entering and leaving these little cars isn't exactly easy. (Author's collection)

One of the most unusual three wheelers, the Frisky was also built as a four-wheeler. Styled by Giovanni Michelotti, of Triumph Herald fame, the Frisky was built in Wolverhampton by Henry Meadows, the engine supplier. Bodies were constructed from glass fibre with an Excelsior 246cc twin engine sitting in the tail. A Villiers 197cc engine was also specified. (Author's collection)

The Velorex, with its tubular structure and canvas bodywork, comes from Czechoslovakia. It first made an appearance in 1954 and remained in production until 1971. Despite its looks it performed well courtesy of 250cc or 350cc Jawa engines. The majority of cars were finished in a reddish-brown colour and were extremely basic. (Ivana Birkettova)

Few Velorex cars have found their way to the United Kingdom and in their native country are sought after by enthusiasts. Travelling in an example is a curious experience, which some would regard as being an acquired taste! (Ivana Birkettova)

A variety of three wheelers are 2CV based, one of the more popular being the Blackjack Avion which is supplied in kit form. Customers obviously need to have some technical expertise and plenty of enthusiasm when building such cars. In the background can be seen a display of Bond Bugs. (Author's collection)

A number of sports three wheelers have been designed in recent years but few have enjoyed such a following as Lomax. The concept was simple: find a sturdy chassis, fit to it a motorcycle or similar engine with suitable transmission, and encase it with a lightweight injection moulded plastic body. The Citroën 2CV chassis with its air-cooled flat-twin 602cc engine and four-speed gearbox proved ideal, and what's more the engine, with its cylinder heads and alloy cooling fins exposed, gives Morgan appeal. (Author's collection)

The 2CV chassis with its soft suspension provides a ride that is altogether uncommon for an open two-seater three wheeler. The 602cc engine affords frugal motoring and is both reliable and easy to maintain. (Author's collection)

The Blackjack Avion's 2CV running gear is highly regarded for its ruggedness and longevity thanks to air-cooling and minimal maintenance requirements. In addition to providing leisurely motoring, the Avion is adept when it comes to participating in motor sport events and hill climbs. (Author's collection)

Sir Clive Sinclair's C5 electric three wheeler made an impact when it was introduced in January 1985. Despite some potential it was an unmitigated disaster, with local authorities banning them on grounds they posed danger to other road users. Entirely exposed to the elements, C5s had to be pedal-assisted up hills as motors lacked sufficient power. C5s were built by Hoover and failed, not surprisingly, to achieve anywhere near anticipated sales. (Author's collection)

Appearing more like a tricycle seen at a holiday complex, the French-built Microcar affords only the barest weather protection. Obviously intended for fine weather use, can this really provide serious motoring? (National Motor Museum)

Three Wheelers

The French produced innumerable microcars in the Seventies and Eighties which afforded minimal motoring for the least expense. They benefited from tax concessions and, in some instances, could be driven without a driving licence. The Arola was one of the more successful designs and was little more than a three wheeled motor scooter with a 47cc Sachs engine driving the rear wheels. (Author's collection)

The Charly Camel was built in Italy, at Pianoro, by All Cars between 1978 and 1985. The design was first shown by Autozodiaco in 1974 and was an advantage in some of Italy's congested cities. (Author's collection)

Microtrucks like this street-worn Vins Nicholas delivery vehicle are ideal in Paris and other cities where parking space is at a premium. Parked behind the minitruck is a Fiat 500 Nuova, the Italian minicar that achieved sales worldwide and which is now very collectable. (Author's collection)

Vespa three wheeler commercials found popularity in France where this example was pictured at Dol de Bretagne. They offer realistic carrying capacity with low running costs, the engine being only 49cc capacity. (Author's collection)

Three Wheelers

Right and on the next page: Seen on mainland Europe over a number of years, Piaggios are now finding a market in Britain where once they would have been derided. Ironically, in concept they are similar to those simple yet sturdy Reliants that first appeared pre-war. Marketed as the Ape 50, these stylish little vehicles are powered by 49.8cc single-cylinder air-cooled two-stroke engines which can return 90mpg. Steering is by handlebars, and there is four-speed transmission; rear brakes are hydraulic and foot applied, while the front is hand-operated. Pick-ups have a payload of 200kg and vans a useful 170kg. Launched at a price under £3000 plus VAT, the potential for Piaggios is enormous. Special equipment is a feature of Piaggios which range from ice cream vending to coffee and catering vehicles, refuse collection to fish and fruit and vegetable sales. (Piaggio publicity material, Author's collection)

Flower Power! Looking the worse for wear, this Piaggio was pictured in Italy where these vehicles are popular because of their versatility and low running costs. (David Herrod)

Three Wheelers

Below: The Micro was an adventurous attempt to change the face of the three wheeler. With its automatic tilting mechanism to enable greater stability, this was viewed as being the way forward in fuel-saving commuter transport or city car. Like many good ideas concepts like this require substantial investment and marketing but do not always come to fruition. (Author's collection)

Above: The car of the future? In April 2002 Volkswagen unveiled its 1-Litre prototype car, so named because it covers 100 kilometres on 1 litre of diesel. It made its road-going debut when Ferdinand Piëch, chairman of VW's board of management, drove the 230km from Wolfsburg to Hamburg at an average speed of 75km/h using only 2.1 litres of fuel thus realising fuel consumption of 0.89litre per 100km. At a mere 1.25m wide, 3.65m long, just over a 1m high and weighing only 290kg, the car's shape was compared with that of the Messerschmitt. (Volkswagen)

Index